*****

S.M.A.R.T.
COUPON SHOPPING
WORKBOOK

*****

Kristie Hammonds

Inspire Publications

A Division of

Inspire Consultants

For information about special discounts for bulk purchases, please contact sales@inspireconsultants.com

Inspire Consultants can bring this author to your live event. For more information or to book an event contact speakers@inspireconsultants.com

ISBN-10:0615477690
ISBN-13:978-0615477695

Table of Contents

Introduction

*****

COUPON SHOPPING FOR LIFE
S.M.A.R.T Coupon Shopping

Welcome to Coupon Shopping for Life!!! You are about to learn how to use your hard earned money to provide more for your family!

This workbook is designed to help you have a clear and easy strategy to save money at the grocery store! You will be a S.M.A.R.T coupon S.T.A.R in no time. However, the real success will come after you go to the store and show what you have learned. Imagine the feeling you will have when you walking out saving more than 50% on your total grocery bill.

In this workbook, you will learn how to maximize every dollar that you spend at the grocery store. We will share with you the exciting ways that you will be able to get a lot of items for FREE! You will be amazed how much money you will save on groceries and everyday items just by spending a little time preparing for your shopping trips.

You will have ideas and strategies to help you prepare healthy and inexpensive meals for your family. You will see how important it is to have a budget in mind for your groceries so that you never overspend again!

These lessons have the potential to be life changing. It is the goal of this program to add value to your life, so that you can truly *Spend Less and Live More*!

Section One

*****

Myth Busting

Myth Busting!!!!!!!

Myth #1: *It takes too much time to coupon shop.*

Reality:

____

Myth #2: *They don't make coupons for anything that we need, use, or that is healthy.*

Reality:

____

Myth #3: *I always spend more money when I use coupons than when I just shop.*

Reality:

____

Myth #4: *My family never eats what I buy when I coupon shop and all the food goes to waste.*

Reality:

____

Myth #5: *I can buy store brand for so much less than I can buy name brand even with a coupon.*

Reality:

____

Do you have preconceived notions or thoughts about coupon shopping that need to be BUSTED?

This is the S.M.A.R.T. Coupon Shopping workshop from Coupon Shopping for Life.

S ____

M____

A____

R____

T____

So let's *Save More and Rejoice Together.* Why not save money on your groceries and household products. Who do you benefit by paying high prices for your groceries? Is it your family? Is it the ones that you love? S.M.A.R.T. Coupon Shopping is more than dollars and cents. It's about taking the financial resources that you already have and maximizing them to produce a better life.

I encourage you to look beyond just saving $1.00 on toothpaste. I want you to look at the broad picture of what that $1.00 saved and reallocated will allow you to do. How will it allow you to live more? That is what S.M.A.R.T. Coupon Shopping is really about.

Section Two

*****

Planning: Your Grocery List and Menu

Plan your grocery List and Menu for the week

Menu planning can save you a lot of time and money.

One small change in how you think about menu planning and grocery shopping makes all the difference!

List 5 meals that your family enjoys and that can be prepared in your home.

1.
2.
3.
4.
5.

The 5 steps to maximize savings by menu planning and coupon shopping

1. ____

2. ____

3. ____

4. ____

5. ____

NOTES:

Section Three

*****

Your Grocery Budget

YOUR GROCERY BUDGET

The two pieces of advice that all the financial experts agree on are:

(1) Spend less than you make.

(2) Have a budget.

Some of us have a rough outline of a budget, some of us have a very specific budget that outlines every dollar, and some of us do not have one at all.

When it comes to maximizing grocery shopping, it's imperative that you have a budget.

Take a moment and write down to the best of your knowledge what you think you are spending on groceries and household items. If you know exactly write that down, if you have a close estimate that is ok too, but we need to know where we are starting from so we will know where we are heading.

**Experts say that most families spend about $150 month per person living in the home.

Simple Monthly Budget Equation

$ __________X 52 = __________/12=$____________ This is your monthly budget.

Decide right now the top three things you would do with the money you save from coupon shopping. Let's assume you save 50% of your budget weekly or monthly, for most it will be more, but let's start there.

What will you do with this new found money? How will you begin to *live more*? Perhaps it's the dream vacation you always wanted, maybe you have felt a calling to serve on a mission trip? It might be to break the chains of debt that have you bound. Whatever it is write it down. Even if it seems out of reach for you today, go ahead and write it down. You will be amazed at how fast you will save money, reach your goals and *live more*.

List Your Goals

1. ______________________________

2. ______________________________

3. ______________________________

Attaining these goals is as easy as 1,2,3!

1. ______________________________

2. ______________________________

3. ______________________________

People often say that they want to get started on a fast track. My advice is eat what you already have for the first week and put your weekly grocery money in the other two envelopes right off the bat. Most of us have enough to eat from “our store” for at least a week, we might not like it but we could do it if we had to!

Another way to get ahead on your budget is to have extreme control for one week. When your lunchtime comes around and you are tempted to go out and grab something, be disciplined and eat the lunch you packed yourself and place the $5 to $10 in your grocery budget envelope. This can be difficult, but you will thank me for it as your envelope fills up with money.

NOTES:

Section Four

*****

Stock Pile and Save

Stockpile and Save!!!!

Stockpiling is the art of buying the products you like and use in bulk when they are at their lowest sale prices.

When you see a great sale on green beans, let's say 0.12 cents a can, if your family eats green beans every week, then you better buy as many as you can while they are at that price.

<u>If you are just buying to save money and get a great deal, you are wasting money!!!!</u>

Some items go on sale seasonally. For example, hot dogs, ketchup, mustard, and relish are always at rock bottom prices throughout the summer. Know the sales cycle so you can save even more.

A chest freezer will allow you to really maximize great sales. Buying low and freezing is a fantastic strategy. These freezers come in many sizes and prices vary. A S.M.A.R.T. coupon shopper can easily make the investment up in no time.

You need to have some space to stockpile all these items you are going to get at a great deal. Now that you have a spot in mind, when you start stockpiling, keep it clean and neat!! If you buy thirteen cans of green beans, stack them nice and neat all in a row. Organization is a must to effectively maximize your shopping.

Where could you place your stockpile items?

____

____

Remember to only buy items that you and your family will use. It is so much fun to get items for free or next to nothing, but you are wasting money and storage space if the items you are getting will never be used. Unless your plan is to donate them to help the community, don't buy it!

NOTES:

Section Five

*****

Coupons: The place to find them

COUPONS...... THE PLACE TO FIND THEM!

Of course the best place to get your coupons is in the Sunday paper. It is very important if you are in a small community to get the "big city" newspaper. There are always more coupons in the larger newspapers, but don't forget about your local paper. You may have a local paper that puts coupon inserts in their Wednesday or Friday paper as well. Even though these are smaller inserts they make great additions to your regular Sunday papers.

Where can you find extra coupons?

1. ____

2. ____

3. ____

4. ____

CATALINA Coupons

These special coupons actually print out from the register at your grocery store. They are usually a “bonus” for buying a number of items from a manufacturer.

Printing Money at Home

I know it sounds illegal, but it is not! You can print coupons at home from your computer. If you begin to shift your mind to thinking that coupons are like cash, you will understand why I call this printing money.

There are many places to print coupons form home, websites directly focusing only on coupons, the manufactures website, and of course the product page on Facebook.

There are three major sources for printable coupons on the web:

1.____

2.____

3.____

E-Coupons, couponing with almost no effort

There are two types of e-coupons. The ones that you add to a store loyalty card and ones that you can download to your smart phone and actually scan the barcode at the checkout right from your phone, both are easy and quick to use and can save you a lot of money every shopping trip!

Let's talk about the type that you add to your store loyalty card. There are three main places to get these and load them to your card.

1.____

2.____

3.____

You may even be able to go to your stores website and add e-coupons from your store onto their card as well.

Other types of coupons

Blinkies: These are the coupons in the little red box on the grocery store shelves. Always pick up a couple of these when you see one, the item is typically not on sale when the blinkie is up, but save those coupons, the sale will be coming soon.

Peelies: These are the coupons that are on the products that you pick up to buy. When you find a peelie on a product, do not peel it off unless you are really buying that product. Just think if you were a customer and you picked up a product you needed and could see the outline of the coupon that someone else peeled off, have respect for other shoppers and refrain from peeling off those coupons unless the item is in your basket. Also, make sure that the peelie coupon is a greater value than any paper coupon you may have. Even though they are an exciting and unexpected find, sometimes they are not the best deal out there!

Tear Pads: These are the coupons you see in front of a particular product that usually promote two or three items at the same time. One example of a popular tear pad coupon is KC Masterpiece Barbeque sauce, it is usually found close to the product, but also at the meat department. It is a coupon that you can use if you are buying both meat and the sauce in one trip.

*Please do not take more than your fair share of tear pad coupons; two at the most will be fine. Remember, these are in limited quantity just like all the other coupons out there and they are meant to be used, not stored in your coupon box to expire.

In-Store Booklets: These are found on displays as you enter your grocery store or on fancy product displays in the store. They may be either store or manufacturer coupons but grab a couple and use them; they are typically much better coupons than the ones in the paper.

Home mailed coupons: The most valuable coupons are usually mailed to you from the manufacturer, if you email or call the company they have a very limited number of great coupons for their products, these come in the mail and once you are on the mailing list you will get little surprises from that manufacturer in the mail a few times a year. They love to hear from their customers so email or call and reap the benefits, remember coupons come out of a company's advertising budget so if they can get feedback from satisfied customers, it justifies the expense.

NOTES:

Section Six

*****

Coupon Terminology

Coupon Terminology

When you start couponing and looking at all the different types of coupons, it can be a little overwhelming at first. I have listed below all the different types of coupons out there that I have seen, hopefully this will help you as you begin to use more coupons.

$ off coupons on a specific product: These are the most popular coupons out there. They are for a specified amount off of a certain item. The item is sometimes very specific so remember, if the coupon is only off of American Cheese don't try to use it on Pepper Jack Cheese, chances are it will not work.

Not valid on trial size: Some coupons have size restrictions. The most common is the *not valid on trial size* coupon. Be careful to check to make sure you have the right size to match your coupon.

Buy one Get one Free: You will need to purchase two items but only pay for one of them; the other will be completely free.

*Try to pair these with great *buy one get one* sales and both items will be free.

One coupon per purchase: You can only use one for each item you purchase, this does not mean that you can only buy one product and use one coupon per transaction. If you have twelve coupons and you buy twelve of the same items, you can use them all in one transaction.

Expiration Dates: Most coupons have expiration dates and typically they are valid for approximately forty five days after the coupon is released. Most of the store chains will not accept an expired coupon. Ask your store what their policy is on recently expired coupons.

*Overseas military can use coupons up to six months after the expiration date at overseas commissaries. Go to www.couponsfortroops.com to learn more about this great program and to donate your expired coupons.

NOTES:

Section Seven

*****

Organizing Your Coupons

Organizing your coupons

There are lots of ways to organize coupons; the key is to find the approach that works best for you. Three options to consider:

- Clipping out all coupons
- Clipping out just the coupons that you intend to use
- Leaving the coupon inserts intact, clipping them when you need them.

Whichever approach you choose, there are several things that you can do to ensure that your coupons remain neat and accessible:

1. **Develop a filing system.** Many people organize their coupons by grocery category--dairy, frozen foods, deli, etc. – but it's not the only way to go. Find a filing system that works for you.

2. **Find a container to hold your coupons.** Use a shoebox, a storage container, a coupon wallet or a recipe box – it doesn't matter what you choose – but it's important to have a landing spot for all of those coupons.

   I like to use a box that snaps closed, that way if one of the kids bumps into it, all of my coupons are fine and they stay put.

3. **File coupons the same day you get them.** Okay, so you may not always have time to file your coupons right away, but try to file them as soon as you can. This will prevent them from getting lost, and save you the hassle of having to sort through a big mess of coupons all at once.

Now that all of our coupons are organized, let's start using them......................

NOTES:

Section Eight

*****

Know Your Store Sales

Know your store sales

Now that we know all about coupons, it is so important to know your stores coupon policy and sale cycle. We need to know if the store's sales ad runs from Wednesday to Tuesday or if it is Sunday to Saturday. Knowing this will ensure you don't miss a great sale on an item just because you were one day late for the sale. Also figure out if it really is a one week sale, look closely at those sale tags on the shelves, sometimes stores will have the same sales for three weeks, if you know the sale will continue, it will give you more time to find more coupons.

If the store is out of an item you had on a list, ask for a raincheck for that item. This seems like a bother, but it will give you up to thirty days to find more coupons for that item. Sometimes a raincheck is a great way to save a lot of money. Just be patient and write down items as you shop that the store is out of. After you check out go to the customer service desk and get your rainchecks. It does not take very long, and it can save you a lot of money when this tool is used correctly.

Look for a *reduced for quick sale* section of your store, ask the manager when they usually mark these items down. A great technique for saving money is to have a loose coupon for an item that is on clearance. Just make sure that the item is marked down at least 25%, if not, wait till it is on sale, you will be able to get a better price then.

Remember from the stockpiling section that an item usually goes on sale at least once every twelve weeks. Buy as many items as you need for that time period when the store has their rock bottom price. That way you will not run out and have to pay a premium for those items later.

NOTES:

Section Nine

*****

Marketing Tactics

Don't Fall for Marketing Tactics

Please remember that a grocery store is open to make money, they invest a lot of money for marketing and advertising to get you to come into their stores. Don't fall for some of their tricky marketing tactics!

Some common tactics are.....

- 10 for 10 Sale
- Buy one Get One Sale
- Get a free ticket or music when you spend a certain amount
- Save money on your purchase of gas

*If a store is having a 10 for $10 sale, you can just buy 1 for $1! You don't need to buy 10 of these special sale items, just buy how many you need.

*In most stores a Buy one Get one sale means that each item will ring up at half price, if you only have one coupon or have never tried the item just buy one at half price, use your coupon, and save money. This is a great way to try new products with limited risk.

*This one is tricky, if your store has a sale that says that if you buy 15 participating items you will receive a free movie ticket, that is only a great deal if you go to the movies! If not, don't feel like you need to buy 15 items. Sometimes we get so caught up in this gimmick that we put things in the cart that we don't need, and worse than that they are at full price, just to get "enough" for the special prize. I feel like the marketing people who put these together are the same ones that put a toy in a cereal box and watch it as it flies off the shelves.

*Be careful with the spend $100 and save .10 cents a gallon of gas trick. This sounds great, especially when fuel prices are soaring, but let's think about this one for a minute. Let's pretend you have a 15 gallon gas tank in your car, that means if you are on empty and you fill up you are going to save .10 cents a gallon on 15 gallons which comes out to a savings of $1.50 per fill up. That is great, unless, you could go to another store down the road and get twice as many groceries for that same $100, you would save a lot more than $1.50. Just be careful, don't fall into the marketing trap that the store has laid for you.

Now there are many more marketing tactics out there, but these are a few really popular ones. Stores use placement of food on shelves, fancy displays to catch our eye, and even words like "surprisingly low prices" to trick us into that impulse buy. Just keep your eyes open and watch for "tricks" to get you to buy more. Now you are a S.M.A.R.T coupon S.T.A.R, so you know to keep your eyes open and watch for these tactics, don't give into them, keep to your list and spend less!

What are some of the marketing tactics that have gotten you to spend more?

1.
2.
3.

NOTES:

Section Ten

******

Combining Sales and Your Coupon Together

Combining Sales and Coupons Together

There are a lot of people out there who do not use coupons because they think that they will buy items that they just don't need. Some people clip a few coupons here and there and forget to use them. Some people think that if they buy name brand food they will spend too much money, even with a coupon.

From what you have learned, I trust you can see that using coupons effectively is a completely different mindset, but it is a small shift in thinking that can save at least 50% on our groceries for you and your family.

The first thing that you need to do is have an idea in your mind when you open that sale insert of just what a regular price and a good sale price looks like. There are rock bottom price sheets in the back of this workbook, you may need to add to this list so that you have the rock bottom prices for the items that are right for your family. This will help you out when you are planning your menus and writing out your list to know exactly what you can get at the best prices that week at your store. You will know just how great a deal is and the list will help you feel good about making that purchase.

Start matching coupons to the sale items using the coupon database on the website www.couponshoppingforlife.com and you will be able to know about how much you will spend for an item before you walk into a store.

For example, you may see that toothpaste is on a 10 for $10 sale, you now know that you can just buy one and get it for $1. You look in the database, and see a coupon for .50 cents. You know your store doubles coupons up to .50 cents, so armed with that knowledge you know your toothpaste will be free!!

Remember, you will never purchase something just because you have a coupon for it. At the end of every month you will have extra coupons that you didn't use. This is the goal! If you are using coupons just to use coupons, then you are not saving money like you should be.

Make sure you are only buying items when they at their lowest price and that you are practicing the fine art of stockpiling to make sure you have plenty of items on hand when you need them.

A lot of stores will also run sales when you buy 10 items, you save $5 dollars or when you buy $25 of items that are participating, you will save $10 off your order. These sales are where you can save big. Leverage these sales by preparing for your trip very carefully and enjoy the money you will save.

*A word of caution on these types of sales.......... The lower priced items included in these sales are always the best deals!

If you are saving $5 off of 10 items that works out to a savings of .50 cents an item, so on a $2 item that is great, but on a $6 item, that is not a large discount at all.

You are going to match up coupons on items that are included on these sales just like you would any other sale. So if you have an item included that is on sale for $2 and you have a coupon for $1 off, you know if you buy 10 of the participating items you will receive another .50 cents off, which will make that $2 item only .50 cents!

But the same sale will have a $6 item; in that case, your $1 coupon and .50 cents savings will make the item $4.50, a good deal, but maybe not as much as you could save if you waited till the lowest price sale for that item.

The key here is to watch what you buy, it is not worth buying 10 items to save $5 if the items are not on that great of a sale and you don't need them.

Another type of sale is buy $25 of participating items and save $10 on your next purchase, now this is a great sale and will yield a 40% savings, but that savings will not be realized until your next purchase.

Pretend that your favorite brands of paper towels are on sale for $8.50 for a 12 ct. package and if you purchase $25 you will receive $10 toward your next purchase.

You would buy 3 packages which would come out to $25.50. You would use 3 $1.00 coupons making your total $22.50 plus tax. You would leave the store with three huge packs of paper towels and a Catalina for $10 off your next purchase.

The next day you find out you are in charge of the potluck event at church and know you will need a lot of paper towels. You run back to the store and grab three more packs and use three more coupons and hand the cashier you $10 Catalina. Your total will be $12.50 plus tax.

You will have purchased a total of six huge packs of paper towels for $34.50 plus tax which is $5.75 a pack and you still have $10 to spend on your next order of anything at that store. No matter how you look at it, that is a great deal!

Some tips about these sales........

The type of transaction described above is considered rolling which is allowed everywhere except Walgreens.

The goal of the transaction is to get as many items included in the sale that you have really great coupons for.

Make sure that the combination of items is as close to the "must spend" amount as possible.

These are great sales, but remember you will not realize the greatest savings until you actually use the $10 Catalina. You might not want to roll the Catalina, you might just want to save it till your next regular grocery trip and cut next week's bills by $10.

NOTES:

Section Eleven

*****

How Do I Start???

This all sounds great………….How do I start???

Here is a step by step plan. It is easier to do anything with a plan in mind.

1. Decide your budget.

    A. How much are you spending right now?
    B. How much do you want to spend?

2. Set realistic goals with your budget.

    A. You might have to work for a few weeks to get the program perfect, allow yourself time.
    B. Always keep in mind the three things you are going to do with the extra money.
    C. Remember to save extra money on the side to stockpile in a separate envelope.

3. Organize your coupons.

    A. Find your perfect balance between organization and time invested.

B. Always have a list of coupons accessible through a database so you know where to look.
C. Remember that your organization may change a time or two before you get your way.

4. Have a price list of lowest prices and prices you have been paying.

   A. Make a list so that when an item goes on sale at 50% off you know it and have the confidence to know it is a great sale.

5. Go through your sale ad to find the lowest priced items in the meat and produce departments. Put the items that are on sale in these departments on your grocery list.

6. With the items you have written down, make a menu for the week.

7. Search your pantry for the rest of the items in the recipes you have chosen. Add any items you may not have for the recipes on your grocery list.

8. Look through your ad to find the best sale items that week and add them to your list.

9. Look at the coupon database on www.couponshoppingforlife.com and match up any coupons to the items you have written down on your list.

10. When you feel discouraged or tired of "doing coupons" take out your folder with receipts that show how much money you have saved and get excited again!

You can feel successful in your couponing efforts if you can step back and say one of two things.........

a. I am saving/spending less on groceries, and I am still providing adequate meals for my family and myself.

b. I am spending about the same at the grocery store, but we are eating healthier and spending more time together as a family because we are not eating out five nights a week.

11. Once your stockpile is where it needs to be; reevaluate your budget and start saving even more. At that point you can begin to maintain your stockpile levels and cut your grocery bill even more.

WARNING:

There are many people who coupon shop that spend way too much money every week. The "good deals" have become addicting and they have a difficult time passing them up. What started out as a blessing has become harmful to them. Remember there is a difference between stockpiling and hording.

I love a bargain, but if you are spending extra money just to get a great deal and not because you need an item in your stockpile, you are actually wasting money. A pantry full of groceries does no good if you are not using the food and you keep buying more and more every week.

NOTES:

Section Twelve

*****

Drug Store Shopping

Drug Store Shopping

I have listed the three major drugstore chains in no particular order. There are hundreds of dollars of "free" items every week at all three. My advice when you are beginning to shop drugstores is to pick one drugstore, preferably closest to home, and just work their plan for a few months. The drugstores are the best places to shop, I rarely need to open my wallet and walk out with a lot of free stuff!!

CVS……

Here is a short guide to help you get started at CVS.

First, CVS has a customer loyalty program called ExtraCare. You will need an extracare card to participate and be able to earn CVS extracare bucks or ECB's. You can get these in the store and start saving money that day. If you already have a card just go online and give them your email address. They will email you a coupon that will get you started, and they will continue to email you coupons every week. You can also scan your card at the red coupon printing kiosk in most stores to get additional coupons. Be sure to scan your card at the beginning of your trip, some of the items on your list might have a coupon print out.

The Extracare system is a customer loyalty program like most grocery stores. You always have to show your extracare card to receive the benefits. The program does not save money off normal prices, it rewards you after your purchase. The reward is the Extracare bucks that print on your receipt that you can then use on your very next purchase.

The products that will print the extracare bucks are listed in your CVS advertisement for the week and will say “free after ECB” or “get $2 ECB back after purchase.

How do I do this??

Here is a short shopping trip to try to explain it easier...

Go into CVS and buy 1 of the free after ECB items. (The first time you do this you will actually pay real money – so for the very first time it is technically not free but from here on it will be.)

You buy Colgate toothpaste for $2.99

You pay $2.99 plus tax (minus your coupon of course)

On your receipt it will print an ECB for $2.99 that you can use on you very next trip.

You can even walk back to the toothpaste aisle grab another Colgate walk up to the counter, hand them your next tube and then your ECB from your last purchase. Your receipt will print another ECB for the same $2.99.

A few tips:

- Make sure you always give them a $$/off $$$ (like the $4 off $20) coupon first before manufacturers coupons
- Always have a list of exactly what is free, sometimes it is very specific items and specific sizes and you want to make sure you are getting the right things.
- Take in a calculator to help you quickly add up your total to make sure you are going to have the right amount for you ECB's to cover it.
- Make sure that what you are buying is equal to your ECB's or a little more. You can pay for $4 worth of items with $5 in ECB but you are throwing money away and you never want to do that.

Here are some commonly ask questions about shopping at CVS.

Isn't CVS really expensive?
Yes, CVS is over-priced on some of their regular priced items. The key to making CVS shopping a wonderful deal is to combine coupons and ECBs.

Rolling ECB

Rolling ECBs means using the ECBs you have already earned to buy items that will give you more ECBs.

Quarterly Extra Care Bucks Too!!!

These are earned based on the amount you actually spent out of pocket at CVS and from prescriptions you've had filled. You will get back 2% of what you actually spent and a $1 ECB for every 2 prescriptions you have filled online or in store.

00-24.99 dollars .... you get $0.00 in ECBs.
25-49.99 dollars .... you get $0.50 in ECBs.
50-74.99 dollars .... you get $1.00 in ECBs.
75-99.99 dollars .... you get $1.50 in ECBs.

The quarters run from January to March, April to June, July to September, and October to December. Your quarterly ECB will print on or after the first day of the month following the end of the quarter.

RITE AID…….

Of the three major drugstores Rite Aid has the most ways to earn their store rewards. There is a basic rebate system that gives you back a set amount on select items called Single Check Rebates, and a fairly new Wellness+ card that earns +UP dollars (similar to Extra Care Bucks from CVS) and other rewards.

Single Check Rebates

Throughout the month Rite Aid will have select items that give a rebate back when you purchase them. The rebate could be the full value of the item or a partial value.

The great part about Rite Aid's program is that you are reimbursed for the full value of the rebate even if you used coupons in the store.

Here is an example:

Benefiber Drink Sticks $7.99

You can use a $2 coupon in store to make the sticks only $5.99, but when you file for your rebate, you will still receive the entire $7.99. In the end you make $2, but it does take some time to get your rebate checks back in the mail, so don't count on the money to pay for your next shopping trip. It will be a nice surprise when it lands in your mailbox!

How do you file for reimbursement?

Go to RiteAid.com and scroll down. You will see a link for Single Check Rebates. Click there and then click to Login. The first time you go here you will need to register, after that your information is stored and you will enter your username and password.

Once you are logged in click to enter a receipt, the system will prompt you to enter a few numbers off the top of your store receipt. After you are done click to save it. You will come back every time you shop and enter another receipt throughout the month. (I usually enter my receipts even if I am not sure if there is a Single Check Rebate available. I have gotten some unexpected ones in the past)

At the end of the month when you are done shopping go back to Rite Aid's site and log in and click to submit your rebates to get your check. They give you a 30 day window after the month ends to ask for your check and then they will mail it out to if you even if you haven't asked yet. It takes about three weeks to receive your check after you request it. Most rebates have a limit of one per household. It could be a rebate period that lasts a week or that lasts the entire month.

Rite Aid Wellness + Program

- You will need to apply for a Wellness+ card when you are in Rite Aid
- Every time you shop have your card scanned before checking out.
- Your card will keep track of your points and extra savings.
- You earn +UP rewards on certain items or purchases.

After you have your card, you will....

Earn 1 point for every dollar spent on non-prescription purchases.

Earn 25 points for every prescription you purchase.

As you earn more points, you earn more rewards!

For every 125 Points	A onetime 10% off shopping pass
500 Points	10% off non-prescription purchase
500 Points	Free Health Screening
1,000 Points	20% off all non-prescription purchases

+UP Rewards

The second reward system at Rite Aid is the new +UP Rewards system. The wellness+ card tracks your purchases and makes +UP rewards print. +UP rewards are Rite Aid money not coupons (just like CVS and Walgreens). So you can use manufacturer coupons and any other store coupons with them.

Commonly Asked Questions

What can I use +UP Rewards on? +UP's can be used on anything in the store except prescriptions, gift cards, tobacco products, alcohol, stamps, or milk.

What is rolling +UP's? Rolling means using the +UP's you have already earned to buy items that will give you more +UP's. You can even use these rewards to pay for items that have Single Check Rebates.

There's a promotion that says I need to buy $20 of products to earn a +UP Reward, is that before or after coupons? Before coupons.

Other Benefits

Exclusive store coupons just for your card!!

Members-only sale pricing throughout the store

10% off Rite Aid Brand products every day

24/7 exclusive access to a pharmacist when you call 1-800-RITEAID

WALGREENS!!!!

Walgreens has a reward system like CVS's, it is an in store coupon called Register Rewards that prints after you buy select products.

Register Rewards

Register rewards are coupons that are printed using the Catalina machines that some grocery stores use. They are Walgreens specific coupons. Register rewards are actually coupons given by the Manufacturers of the products that are on special that week.

For example: You buy Secret deodorant and a $1 Register Reward prints (this register reward is provided by Procter and Gamble). When you use your Register Reward, Walgreens will then submit that coupon to Procter and Gamble and get reimbursed.

Commonly asked questions

- **What makes a Register Reward print**? Register Rewards are linked to specific products each week. Sometimes you only need to buy one item, sometimes it is for buying a certain dollar amount of products.
- **Can I use a Register Reward to buy the same item again? NO!** If you go in and buy an item or items that make a RR print and then you try to use that specific RR again to buy the same items the next RR will not print.
- **Can I use a Register Reward to buy a different Register Reward item or items?** YES! You can "roll" your RR buy using them on a different Register Reward deal. As long as you are not using them on the same products or product brands.
- **How long are Register Rewards good for?** Most are good for 2 weeks some that you get will be good for a shorter amount of time.
- **What if my Register Reward doesn't print?** Call 1-888-8COUPON and talk to the Catalina company and they will mail you the RR that you should have received.

What order should I use my coupons ?

Walgreens computers are programmed not to accept coupons for an item if the coupon is over the price of an item. To help reduce problems use coupons in this order when checking out.

Any $/$$ (like $5 off $20 purchase)

Register Rewards

B1G1 manufacturer coupons

Other Manufacturer coupons

Then Store coupons

Because Register Rewards are a manufacturer coupon the system will kick them out if you have already used a coupon from that manufacturer for that product. If they are not going to allow you to use a coupon, you would rather it not let you use a .50 cent coupon rather than a $10 Register Reward.

Because most Walgreens coupons (the great coupons you can clip from their sale ad) are really price changing codes rather than money off coupons, you want to use these last. You want the computer to “think” the item is full price when you use your manufacturer coupon.

I make my list for Walgreens and then I place my coupons in order of how I am going to hand them to the cashier, I then hand them one at a time to the cashier so I am watching to make sure the order is correct.

Remember Register Rewards have short expiration dates on them, if they expire it is like throwing real money away. If you think you will not use them in the short amount of time you have, march right back into the store and use them that day on household items like milk, paper towels, storage bags, or anything that takes away from your weekly budget!

Walgreens shopping is a lot of fun, but with all the limits, rolling rules, and order of coupons, it is not for a person who is not comfortable with coupons. Make sure; if this is the store you use, be prepared. I typically choose to shop at Walgreens, but it still makes me a little apprehensive. I just know when I am at the checkout, I need to hand the coupons in a certain order and I watch the cash register to make sure I have figured everything correctly.

I hope you have seen in this section on drugstore shopping just how valuable these stores can be. I once thought that anything I purchased at a drugstore was so expensive, but it was because I did not know how to "use" their program. Once I understood the way the stores worked, I have been able to "make money" using all three major drugstores. I truly enjoy shopping at all three of these stores and hope you will enjoy it as well. It is a great feeling to walk out of a store with a cart full of "free" items and have "money" to come back next week.

NOTES:

Section Thirteen

*****

Closing Thoughts

You have made it!!!! You are a S.M.A.R.T. coupon S.T.A.R!!

All that is left is to implement what you have learned and start saving money on your groceries. With this new knowledge and confidence knowing that you are part of a community that is ready to support you. Your ready to Spend Less and Live More!!

I do want to take just a moment to remind each of you that no matter how many sales you go to, how many coupons you use, no matter how many mail in rebates you complete, and no matter how much money you save, always remember that it is Jesus Christ who is the provider of all of our needs. It is he who has offered the greatest savings we will ever receive through his saving grace and eternal salvation.

I hope that this has made a positive impact in your life and that you will leave today armed with the knowledge to always save money on groceries and other household items and to enjoy the life you have been blessed with to the fullest.

Section Fourteen

*****

Additional Resources

Items for Free

There are a few items that you should **Never** pay for!

Refer to this list to know if you are spending money on items that should always be free.

Health and Beauty Items......

- Antacid
- Anti Bacterial Soap
- Bandages
- Body Lotion
- Cough Drops
- Dental Floss
- Deodorant (men's/ women's)
- Mouthwash
- Razors
- Shampoo
- Shaving Cream
- Shower Gel
- Soap
- Toothbrush
- Toothpaste

Household Items………

- Air Freshener(spray)
- Candles
- Cleaning Supplies
- Dish Detergent (liquid)
- Liquid Hand Soup
- Plug in Fresheners

Grocery Items……

- Barbecue Sauce
- Cake Mix
- Canned Biscuits
- Canned Soup
- Chicken broth or Beef Broth
- Cookie Mix
- Frosting
- Frozen Vegetables
- Hot Sauce
- Muffin Mix
- Mustard
- Pouch Tuna and Canned Tuna
- Sour Cream
- Spaghetti
- Tomato Sauce or Paste
- Yogurt

Until you build up your stockpile and your coupons, you may have to pay pennies for these items, but you should never again need to pay full price!

Rock Bottom Prices

These products are at the right buying price; try to build your stockpile so that you will only need to buy these items at these lowest prices available! Prices listed are after coupons.

Meat and Deli Items	
Bacon	**$2.49lb**
Roast Beef	**$2.25 lb**
Beef Steaks	**$4.00lb**
Bone in Chicken Breasts	**$0.99lb**
Bone in Chicken Wings	**$0.79lb**
Deli Meat	**$1.99lb**
Ground Beef	**$1.99lb**
Hot Dogs	**$0.99**
Pork Chops	**$1.69lb**
Pork Loin Roast	**$1.75lb**
Whole Chicken	**$0.89lb**

Fresh Produce	
Apples	$1.00 lb
Bagged Salad, "Fancy Blends"	$2.00
Bagged Salad, Iceberg	$1.00
Bananas	$0.35 lb
Bell Pepper (Green)	$0.49 each
Bell Peppers (Red, Yellow, or Orange)	$0.79 each
Blueberries	$1.50 pint
Broccoli	$1.00 lb
Corn on the Cob	$0.20 each
Cucumbers	$0.50lb
Grapes	$1.25 lb
Lettuce	$1.00 each
Onions	$0.79 lb
Oranges	$0.79 lb
Peaches or Nectarines	$0.79 lb
Red or Gold Potatoes	$2.00/ 5 lb
Russet Potatoes	$2.50/ 10 lb
Strawberries	$1.50/ 16 oz
Watermelon	$2.00
Zucchini or Squash	$0.50 lb

Drinks	
Dry Drink Mixes (Lemonade)	$1.00/ 6 pack container
Fruit Juice	$0.99/ 64 oz.
Kool Aid	$0.10 pack
Orange Juice	$2.69 gal.
Soft Drinks	$0.59/ 2 liter
Soft Drinks	$2.50/ 12 pack cans
Tea Bags (Black)	$0.50/ 40ct.
Tea Bags (Herbal Blends)	$0.50/ 12 ct.

Condiments	
Apple Cider Vinegar	$1.50
Honey	$1.50
Ketchup	$0.50/ 24 oz.
Mayonnaise	$1.29/ 12 oz.
Salad Dressing	$0. 50/ 14 oz
Soy Sauce	$0.89
Worcestershire Sauce	$0.50

Dairy	
Milk	$2.69 gal.
Eggs	$1.19 doz.
Cheese Slices	$1.50 / 16 slices
Butter	$1.50 lb
Cream Cheese	$0.69 / 8 oz
Refrigerated Biscuits	$0.40

Frozen Foods	
Chicken Breasts	$4.00 Bag
Chicken Strips	$3.50
Entrees	$1.00 Single Serve
French Fries	$2.00
Ice Cream	$2.00
Juice Concentrate	$0.75
Pizza	$3.00

Canned and Dry Goods	
Bagels	$1.50 / 6 ct.
Boxed Meal Kits	$0.70
Buns	$1.00 / 8 ct.
Canned Chicken	$1.00 each
Canned Fruit	$0.50 / 15 oz.
Canned Tomatoes	$0.50 / 15oz.
Canned Vegetables	$0.50
Cereal	$.85 - $1.25
Cookies	$0.79 package
Crackers	$1.00 package
Jell-O	$0.35
Macaroni and Cheese	$0.40
Most Spices	$1.00
Nuts	$0.89 container
Oatmeal	$0.89
Pancake Mix	$1.00
Pasta Sauce	$.50 / 24 oz
Popcorn	$0.75-1.25 / 6 pack microwave bag
Rice	$0.90 per pound
Tortillas	$1.25 doz.

Baking Goods	
Baking Powder	$1.00
Baking Soda	$0.89
Brown Sugar	$0.75 / 2lb
Chocolate Chips	$0.75 bag
Cocoa	$2.50
Cooking Oil Spray	$1.25
Cornstarch	$1.00
Flour	$2.00 / 5lb
Sugar	$2.00 / 4 lb
Vanilla Flavoring	$1.50
Vegetable Oil	$1.50 bottle

House Hold Goods	
Bleach	$0.75
Dishwasher Detergent	$1.00 / 20 tabs
Dryer Sheets	$2.00
Foil	$0.89
Freezer Bags	$1.00
Glass Cleaner	$0.50
Laundry Detergent	$2.50 / 32 loads
Paper Towels	$3.50 / 8 roll pack
Sandwich Bags	$1.00
Storage Bags	$1.00
Toilet Bowl Cleaner	$0.50
Toilet Paper	$2.50 / 9 roll
Trash Bags	$3.50

For additional resources visit

www.couponshoppingforlife.com

To assist you further in your money saving efforts we have assembled hundreds of E-Books in multiple categories such as Cooking, Gardening, Finance, Personal Growth and Health and Fitness. These books are available to you at 70-90 % off retail prices.

New titles are added to the selection weekly so check in often!

Bring the S.M.A.R.T Coupon Shopping workshop to your community. These workshop are an ideal fundraising opportunity for your church, school or charity. For more information call

Toll Free 888-406-0668

or email
workshop@couponshoppingforlife.com

Spend Less, Live More

Made in the USA
Monee, IL
08 November 2026

68020214R00070